Monday Motivations

Pastor Rachel Blankenship

Copyright © 2022 Rachel Blankenship
All rights reserved.
ISBN:9798405753973

THE HOLY BIBLE, NEW INTERNATIONAL VERSION®, NIV® Copyright © 1973, 1978, 1984, 2011 by Biblica, Inc.® Used by permission. All rights reserved worldwide.

Welcome friends!

This is a book full of a years' worth of Monday Motivations!

Mondays can be tough, oftentimes they are even dreaded! So each week, you can open your book and allow God's word to shift your perspective! I hope to use the word to help you see the gratitude in having a relationship with Jesus, an encouragement to stand firm in the things of God and inspire you to expand your thoughts on sharing Him to those around you!

Each Monday morning, you can grab your coffee and open your book! You will find a topic of focus, three scriptures along with a motivational message to spark a great start to the week!

~Love and Blessings~

Psalm 5:3
"In the morning, Lord, you hear my voice; in the morning I lay my requests before you and wait expectantly."

Week 1

Happy Monday! Today I want to give you the encouragement to open your mind and heart to receive the renewal that the Lord wants to give you each day. It should be our desire to continue to grow personally as well as spiritually, even though it may look differently than we expect at times.

The Word says in:

Romans 12: 2-

"Do not conform to the pattern of this world, but be transformed by the renewing of your mind. Then you will be able to test and approve what God's will is—his good, pleasing and perfect will."

Colossians 3:10-

"and have put on the new self, which is being renewed in knowledge in the image of its Creator."

Philippians 4:8-

"Finally, brothers and sisters, whatever is true, whatever is noble, whatever is right, whatever is pure, whatever is lovely, whatever is admirable—if anything is excellent or praiseworthy—think about such things."

We all find ourselves in need of being refreshed or maybe even a fresh start all together.. However, a fresh start isn't always a place or a destination. It can be a mindset. God wants us to have a fresh start to the day, a fresh outlook on what He has for us to do, and a renewed focus on the "big picture". In order to do that and not face burnout, you must stay connected to your creator. When you spend time with Him, time in the word and remain focused on the "things above", you will experience change! It will allow you to experience growth in knowledge, change in your way of thinking, a shift in your perspective as well as allowing you to be refreshed every single day!

God is faithful! His supply is endless and He will not abandon nor forsake you! If you will reach out to Him, He will show up day after day and give you all that you need for the moment at hand. Dig in, connect with Him, allow Him to renew your mind, and transform your life, one day at a time!

Love y'all,

Have a blessed week!

Week 2

Happy Monday! Today I want to give you the motivation and encouragement to love when it is tough! We all have encountered people in life who have been unpleasant to us, hurt us in some way or may just not be our favorite person. Allow God to help you heal and still see them with love. You don't want to block a blessing that God has for you because you are still holding on to a past experience.

The Word says in:

Matthew 5:44-

"But I tell you, love your enemies and pray for those who persecute you,"

Matthew 6:14-15

"For if you forgive other people when they sin against you, your heavenly Father will also forgive you. But if you do not forgive others their sins, your Father will not forgive your sins."

Ephesians 4:31-32

"Get rid of all bitterness, rage and anger, brawling and slander, along with every form of malice. Be kind and compassionate to one another, forgiving each other, just as in Christ God forgave you."

Remember that hurting people often hurt people and lost people are not going to conduct themselves in a way that saved people would. It's ok.

Stay open to pray for those who live differently from you, even those who have wronged you. You may need to have firm boundaries with them but don't close your heart. Try to remember that even though they may be lost and broken...they are still God's children and He still loves them. Don't harden your heart and refuse to intercede in prayer on their behalf. If the Lord brings it to you or lays it on you, put your personal emotions aside, allow yourself to see them as His child and pray for them.

Love y'all,

Have a blessed week!

Week 3

Happy Monday! Today I want to give you the motivation to not get distracted by your own wants! It seems like a crazy thought right? We are usually taught that it is our desires and dreams that should be what motivates us, but sometimes we can let it distract us from the things God has for us.

The Word says in:

Acts 1:7-

"He said to them: "It is not for you to know the times or dates the Father has set by his own authority."

Ecclesiastes 3:1-

"There is a time for everything, and a season for every activity under the heavens"

Psalm 27:14-

"Wait for the Lord; be strong and take heart and wait for the Lord."

It can be easy sometimes to get caught up in our desires, our thoughts, our plans and our ways. If we aren't careful, we can miss valuable lessons and waste valuable time being preoccupied with "our" plans. I encourage you all to not allow yourself to be sidetracked by your own ideas. Don't rush things to suit your wants.

God's plans were set in motion before we even had the thought of what was ahead and His timing is always perfect! We don't have to spend our time being anxious, trying to force things or trying to figure out all of the answers. Instead, we can rest in Him. We can trust that each season we are in is purposeful and what He has spoken over us will come to pass at just the right time!

Love y'all,

Have a blessed week!

Week 4

Happy Monday! Today I want to give you the encouragement to not be held back by things that are in your past. Instead, I hope to inspire you to embrace the new life that God provides you with!

The Word says in:

Isaiah 43:18-19-

"Forget the former things; do not dwell on the past. See, I am doing a new thing! Now it springs up; do you not perceive it? I am making a way in the wilderness and streams in the wasteland."

2 Corinthians 5:17-

"Therefore, if anyone is in Christ, the new creation has come: The old has gone, the new is here!"

Ezekiel 36:26-

"I will give you a new heart and put a new spirit in you; I will remove from you your heart of stone and give you a heart of flesh."

There are so many times in our lives, where we hold ourselves back from walking in the fullness of what God has for us to do. We all have a mission specially designed just for us! Unfortunately, we can often feel unworthy, based on our past decisions or dealings.

The truth is, that once we are born again with Jesus, He removes all of that. It is gone! We no longer have to be bound or held back by past hurts, guilt, shame, or regret. Jesus gave us freedom from those things! He knew who you were when He created you and when He placed your purpose within you. Let Him give you your identity! Accept who He says you are and begin to see yourself how He sees you!

Look forward! Take this new day, new week and walk in the newness of life that walking with God provides!

Love y'all,

Have a blessed week!

Week 5

Happy Monday! This morning I wanted to take a moment to motivate you to stop trying to handle things all on your own! You don't have to! You have the greatest help you could ever need and He is with you all the time!

The Word says in:

Matthew 19:26-

"Jesus looked at them and said, "With man this is impossible, but with God all things are possible."

Isaiah 41:10-

"So do not fear, for I am with you; do not be dismayed, for I am your God. I will strengthen you and help you; I will uphold you with my righteous right hand."

Philippians 4:13-

"I can do all this through him who gives me strength."

It's a new day, a fresh start to the week and you don't have to walk, fix, solve, heal things all on your own. You have a Savior who is right beside you! He is waiting for you to give Him the opportunity to work in your life and in your situations. God cares about the things that you care about. God cares about the things that you are concerned about. And He wants to help!

He can move mountains. He can give peace and joy beyond understanding. He is a God who can make a way out of no way, make dry bones live, and can break the chains that are holding us bound!

The Bible doesn't say, you can handle anything you face, but it does say that "with God, all things are possible"! I encourage you today to lay the things that you have been carrying at His feet. Let it go! Let God do what He does! When we move ourselves out of the way, He can step in and do His greatest works! You are not abandoned in your situation. You are not forsaken along this journey. He is there going before you, walking beside you and watching your back!

Take the opportunity of this new week and decide to take a new path! Turn things over to Jesus and allow Him to work! He will give you strategies for everything He brings you to...and if you listen, you will learn, grow and appreciate Him in a deeper way when you are on the other side!

Love y'all, have a great week!

Week 6

Happy Monday! This week I wanted to talk to you guys about living every moment fully! A lot of us are living, but are you living fully?

In the Word it says:

Psalm 90:12-

"Teach us to number our days, that we may gain a heart of wisdom."

James 4:14-

"Why, you do not even know what will happen tomorrow. What is your life? You are a mist that appears for a little while and then vanishes."

Colossians 3:23-

"Whatever you do, work at it with all your heart, as working for the Lord, not for human masters,"

Most of us have had the realization at some point of another that time is short, but if we aren't careful and we don't live intentionally, it can be easy sometimes to take it for granted. When we get a full revelation that we don't have much time here (even if we get 110 years, it isn't long) and that we never know what tomorrow will bring, it should light a fire under us to live more fully each and every day. There is not one day to be wasted!

It should also cause us to live more fully for God. Our heart's posture every day should be: to operate from a space where our hearts long to do ALL things as we are doing all of them for Him. We should have our ears and hearts turned to Him in such a way that we not only hear from Him, but we do all the things He asks us to do with urgency.

God created you with a specific purpose in mind that only you can fulfill. There will never be another you, and you don't get a second chance. So live wisely. Live intentionally, don't waste an opportunity, and stay busy living for Him!

Love y'all!

Have a blessed week!

Week 7

Happy Monday! This week I want to talk to you about connection! We are meant to connect! Connection is where we gain our strength, our encouragement and added support. It is how we feed into each other and continue God's work from generation to generation!

The Word says in:

Genesis 2:18-

"The Lord God said, "It is not good for the man to be alone. I will make a helper suitable for him."

1 Corinthians 12:26-

"If one part suffers, every part suffers with it; if one part is honored, every part rejoices with it."

Proverbs 27:17-

"As iron sharpens iron, so one person sharpens another."

We were created to connect with one another! Throughout the Bible there are verses about the importance of connection. God never designed us to walk this journey alone. We were meant to walk alongside Him and build relationships with one another. We were created to connect so that we can encourage one another, build each other up, support each other in tough times, help hold each other accountable and help teach each other lessons He has given us.

The people we surround ourselves with are important, they make an impact! Be sure as you go through life, that you continue to build your relationship with God. Also, be sure that you build a circle of friends who are rooted in the word. Find a church that preaches the word and who will come alongside you and walk through life with you.

Make sure your relationships are ones that bring you closer to God and glorify Him. Ensure that you are continuously connecting with God each day so that you can also be that Godly friend and influence the people around you.

Love y'all!

Have a blessed week!

Week 8

Happy Monday! This week, I want to spend some time talking to you all about loving your neighbor and loving yourself! Both can be challenging or even feel foreign, but both are so important!

The Word says in:

Psalm 139:13-15-

"For you created my inmost being; you knit me together in my mother's womb. I praise you because I am fearfully and wonderfully made; your works are wonderful, I know that full well. My frame was not hidden from you when I was made in the secret place, when I was woven together in the depths of the earth."

John 13:34-35-

"A new command I give you: Love one another. As I have loved you, so you must love one another. By this everyone will know that you are my disciples, if you love one another."

1 Corinthians 16:14-

"Do everything in love."

God made you unique and uniquely qualified to do and be what He has created for you to be or do. He made you, on purpose and with a purpose.

He loves us in such an amazingly unconditional and gracious way! He calls us to love each other as He loves us , but we cannot really love each other the way He loves us until we truly accept His love for us. When we get a revelation of His love and we begin to walk in it, the way that we love other people will change. We will have a greater capacity to love others and will have the ability to share all things in truth but seasoned with love.

The closer we get to Him, the more we accept His love for us. The more we accept and fill ourselves with His love for us, the more of His love we can share with other people and we will be able to operate, more fully, in the ways that He wants us to!

Love y'all!

Have a blessed week!

Week 9

Happy Monday! Today, I want to talk to you guys about standing in the LIGHT! There is darkness in the world, there are dark moments that we may walk through, but as a child of God, you have The Light inside of you and when The Light shows up, all darkness has to flee!

The Word says in:

Genesis 1:4-

"God saw that the light was good, and he separated the light from the darkness."

John 1:4-

"In him was life, and that life was the light of all mankind."

Ephesians 5:8-

"For you were once darkness, but now you are light in the Lord. Live as children of light"

You may have heard it talked about before that we are to be a light in this dark world. But it is so important to decide and know where you stand. If you see the world around you getting darker, what do you do? Do you join in? Are you overcome by it? Do you lose the hope you have in the Lord? We as Christians are warned in the Bible over and over again about being on guard. It is something that has been and continues to be vital.

Darkness is going to come, we are going to see schemes of the enemy rise up. These are facts that we know, however, it is our response that is important. How we handle it when it comes is what will make the difference. Are we standing as pillars of light, as lighthouses in the darkness? That is what we are called to do. So I encourage you this week to take a look at where you are. Have you made up your mind to stand against the darkness? Make the decision that no matter what may come, you will stand in His light, in His hope, in His strength.

Love y'all!

Have a blessed week!

Week 10

Happy Monday! In a world that can be so uncertain, it can be hard to focus on the bigger picture. So I wanted to take a moment and give you a little encouragement. No matter what is happening around us, no matter what has happened in our past, we can continue to move forward in peace, knowing that we are in alignment with our God given mission. Don't forget that you were created on purpose and for a direct purpose to be carried out while you are here.

The Word says in:
Colossians 3:2-
"Set your minds on things above, not on earthly things."

Proverbs 4:25-27-
"Let your eyes look straight ahead; fix your gaze directly before you. Give careful thought to the paths for your feet and be steadfast in all your ways. Do not turn to the right or the left; keep your foot from evil."

1 Peter 5:8-
"Be alert and of sober mind. Your enemy the devil prowls around like a roaring lion looking for someone to devour."

The enemy is out here lurking, prowling and ready to destroy anyone he can. He will fill you with shame about your past decisions, he will make you feel unworthy of accomplishing anything for God. If that doesn't work, he will begin to throw things into your life to distract you from your purpose or even from your relationship with God.

I encourage you this week to really focus on the things of heaven. Know what your God given purpose is and commit to it. If you haven't found it, pray about it, seek clarity.

Allow the Lord to direct your path and renew your mind today and every day going forward so that you may not be distracted but stay in alignment no matter what life may bring your way!

Love y'all!

Have a blessed week!

Week 11

Happy Monday! This week, I want to encourage you to watch your words! They hold power! As believers, we must be careful of the words that we speak and allow ourselves to be led by the Spirit in what to say and what to edit.

The Word says:
Proverbs 18:21-
"The tongue has the power of life and death, and those who love it will eat its fruit."

2 Timothy 2:16-
"Avoid godless chatter, because those who indulge in it will become more and more ungodly."

Matthew 12:36-
"But I tell you that everyone will have to give account on the day of judgment for every empty word they have spoken."

Our words hold tremendous power and have definitive consequences. It is our daily choice in how we choose to use them.

The Word tells us that foolish talk influences more ungodly behavior. Foolish talk can include talking negatively about another person or spreading information about another person that isn't true or may even be hurtful. Instead of spending your time with worthless talk, set your mind on building up one another.

Choose to use your words to build people up and encourage those around you. Be a light for others, not someone who tears them down and makes them feel less than. Speaking life over yourself and those around you will be far more rewarding, and it will lead to a greater sense of inner peace. Give it a try!

Love y'all!

Have a blessed week!

Week 12

Happy Monday! I wanted to talk to you guys this morning about giving God our all! Sometimes that can be tough, but it is so vital to our experience and our purpose!

In the Word it says:

2 Kings 4:3-4-

"Elisha said, "Go around and ask all your neighbors for empty jars. Don't ask for just a few. 4 Then go inside and shut the door behind you and your sons. Pour oil into all the jars, and as each is filled, put it to one side."

James 4:10-

"Humble yourselves before the Lord, and he will lift you up."

Proverbs 23:26-

"My son, give me your heart and let your eyes delight in my ways,"

God wants us to give all we have. He wants us, all of us, every crevice and fiber of our beings. He wants it! He wants us to trust Him enough to humble ourselves before Him, give Him our whole hearts and be willing to listen and go where He leads.

God can't fulfill His purpose for you if you aren't willing to walk in His ways. He can't fill what you won't offer. He can't bless what you won't give Him control of. So I encourage you this week to let God have total access, give Him all of it.

Let Him search you. Let Him show you areas you've been holding back. Let Him reveal the vessels you've withheld and any of His ways you haven't been listening to. Let His unfailing love break open the hidden places of your heart and fill them with Him. God wants to do great things for you and through you, but He can only use what you are willing to give. Trust Him. Open your heart and mind to all He has for you!

Love y'all
Have a blessed week!

Week 13

Good Morning! This week I want to evaluate your hearts and see if there is anything that is holding you back from fully accepting the love of God? You are so unbelievably loved!

The Word says:

John 3:16-

"For God so loved the world that he gave his one and only Son, that whoever believes in him shall not perish but have eternal life."

Romans 5:8-

"But God demonstrates his own love for us in this: While we were still sinners, Christ died for us."

Romans 8:37-39-

"No, in all these things we are more than conquerors through him who loved us. For I am convinced that neither death nor life, neither angels nor demons, neither the present nor the future, nor any powers, neither height nor depth, nor anything else in all creation, will be able to separate us from the love of God that is in Christ Jesus our Lord."

Take a moment and re-read those scriptures, really immerse yourself in them. When you do, you will see just how much you are loved! Oh my goodness, how amazingly, unconditionally, and completely loved we are by our Lord!

We are so loved, we were worth God sending His son. We are so loved that Jesus was willing to step out of heaven and into time to be with us, give us an earthly example and to lay down His life all just to have us in heaven with Him! How amazing is that! Even more beautiful is the fact that the word says not only are we loved that much, at the worst of our worst, He loved us that much. Even further, there is NOTHING that can separate us. He loves us that much!

Unfortunately, there are so many times that we can "know" the verses, we can know we are loved, but we still have things within us that causes us to not fully accept this great love that He has for us. So this week, I encourage you to go to God and let Him reveal the reasons to you, allow Him to release healing into those places, and truly allow yourself to experience the fullness of His love!

Love y'all! Have a blessed week!

Week 14

Happy Monday! During this week I just want you to really focus on the gift that we were given so many years ago, in the birth of Jesus. It isn't something to only celebrate once a year. It should be something we are grateful for everyday!

The Word says:

James 1:17-

"Every good and perfect gift is from above, coming down from the Father of the heavenly lights, who does not change like shifting shadows."

Romans 6:23-

"For the wages of sin is death, but the gift of God is eternal life in Christ Jesus our Lord."

John 4:10-

"Jesus answered her, "If you knew the gift of God and who it is that asks you for a drink, you would have asked him and he would have given you living water."

The word says that every good and perfect gift is from above and I cannot think of a better or more perfect gift than Jesus. He was willing to come down from heaven, be born in a lowly place, live a blameless life as our example and give everything He had just to be with us!

According to the word, we all deserve death and eternal separation. There is nothing we could ever do "good enough" to earn our way into heaven. But He loves us so much that He was willing to give it all to tear the veil. He breaks down the barriers to have a personal relationship with us while we are here, and welcomes us into heaven when we get there!

If we choose to be, we can be full of His living water and experience His promises and will for us daily, even this side of heaven. I don't know about you, but I am thankful everyday for a God that loves me enough to be ever-present! I don't have to wait on a certain day or person to be available. I don't have to perform a ceremony and "hope" it was good enough. I can access heaven anytime of the day or night. I have FULL access to a God that loves me, wants the best for me and knows how to guide and protect me along that path. What a gift! Spend some time this week, appreciating and utilizing the great gift you have been given! Love y'all, Have a Blessed Week!

Week 15

Happy Monday! This morning I want to talk to you guys about choosing wisely! Our choices and the people we choose to do life with, can affect the trajectory of our lives, either for the good or not so great. It is important that we use wisdom in making those decisions.

The Word says in:
Proverbs 13:20-
"Walk with the wise and become wise, for a companion of fools suffers harm."

Proverbs 27:17-
"As iron sharpens iron, so one person sharpens another."

Proverbs 12:26-
"The righteous choose their friends carefully, but the way of the wicked leads them astray."

The people you choose to be surrounded by and those you allow to speak into your life are so important! The Bible gives guidance about this over and over again! Choose wisely!

The people that you spend the most time with are the ones who have the greatest impact on your thoughts/thought processes, your attitude, your actions, your decisions and your beliefs.

Surround yourself with people who are wise and will give you wise counsel. Surround yourself with those who speak life into and over things that come up. Surround yourself with friends who will pray for you and encourage you with the word. Surround yourself with people who can see the greatness that God places within you and want you to live up to that potential.....but don't stop there! Also choose to be that kind of person to the ones who look to you as a friend!

Love y'all!

Have a great week!

Week 16

Happy Monday! A new month, a new week or even a new day, can be a great thing! It can be an exciting time for looking towards new things! No matter what this new time holds, God gave me a reminder to share with you: He has you!

The Word says:

Romans 8:28-

"And we know that in all things God works for the good of those who love him, who[a] have been called according to his purpose."

Jeremiah 29:11-

"For I know the plans I have for you," declares the Lord, "plans to prosper you and not to harm you, plans to give you hope and a future."

Psalm 16:8-

"I keep my eyes always on the Lord. With him at my right hand, I will not be shaken."

In this fallen world, everything will not be perfect all the time, but because you have the power of a resurrected Jesus on the inside, you can walk through it with victory and you can trust the one who is holding you! He knows every moment of time from beginning to end. There is nothing that occurs that He is surprised by.

Even more than that, everything He allows or you step into, He can use! Isn't that something? God can even use something that the enemy intended to harm you and bring good from it! That is the God we serve! He has a good plan for your life, purpose He has placed inside of you and a hope for your future.

His plan for your life is not to harm you, it is to give you a greater life! So in the mountaintop moments, praise Him for His provision. In the valleys, press in, listen, grow closer to Him. Keep your heart turned to Him, so that He can reveal to you the lessons and goodness that He wants to bring from it all!

Love y'all
Have a blessed week!

Week 17

Happy Monday! Today I want to encourage you to not be overcome with darkness but instead, be the light shining in the darkness!

The Word says in:

John 8:12-

"When Jesus spoke again to the people, he said, "I am the light of the world. Whoever follows me will never walk in darkness, but will have the light of life."

Matthew 5:16-

"In the same way, let your light shine before others, that they may see your good deeds and glorify your Father in heaven."

Genesis 7:1-

"The Lord then said to Noah, "Go into the ark, you and your whole family, because I have found you righteous in this generation."

We live in a fallen world. There are times that we can see the darkness more so than others, but since the fall of Adam and Eve, it has been part of this world. Over the past year especially, we have been able to see the darkness, but we are not without hope! The Lord is the light of this world and He uses us as vessels of His light to a dark and hurting world.

In Noah's day, the world was full of darkness. He and his family were the only ones who were living for God! Could you imagine? As dark as it is right now, there are still more than one of us living sold out for Jesus! When God sees a righteous heart, He honors that. Through our obedience and relationship with Him, we can glorify Him for all that He is to the people of this world!

So I encourage you all to not be overcome or distracted by the darkness of the world. Instead, lean in to God, and let Him fill you with His light. When you do, you will be able to share His light with everyone you interact with and be a vessel of light in the darkness.

Love y'all! Have a blessed week!

Week 18

Good morning everyone and Happy Monday! Today I want to talk to you about growth!

The Word says:

Jeremiah 12:2- *"You have planted them, and they have taken root; they grow and bear fruit. You are always on their lips but far from their hearts."*

Psalm 92:12-14- *"The righteous will flourish like a palm tree, they will grow like a cedar of Lebanon; planted in the house of the Lord, they will flourish in the courts of our God. They will still bear fruit in old age, they will stay fresh and green,"*

2 Peter 1:5-8- *"For this very reason, make every effort to add to your faith goodness; and to goodness, knowledge; and to knowledge, self-control; and to self-control, perseverance; and to perseverance, godliness; and to godliness, mutual affection; and to mutual affection, love. For if you possess these qualities in increasing measure, they will keep you from being ineffective and unproductive in your knowledge of our Lord Jesus Christ."*

It is so important that we remain mindful of where our roots are planted and that we continue to seek growth. It can be easy to be thrown off track, however, that is why it is vital that we stay connected to God and His word every day! Not just going through the motions just to check a box. Instead, we need to truly come to Him to seek His presence.

We need to seek a word from Him, to get encouragement and perspective. Your walk was never meant to be a "one-time" act. God wants you to grow and mature in the ways of Him. He wants you to grow and become sturdy in your faith, sturdy in His word! I encourage you this week to come to your time with Him with fresh eyes and a fresh heart.

Allow Him to open your mind and give you a fresh hunger for all of the things of Him: His word, His ways and His will!

Love y'all! Have a great week!

Week 19

Happy Monday everybody! I hope your week is starting off well! Today, I want to talk to you about standing.

The Word says:

Ephesians 6:11-

"Put on the full armor of God, so that you can take your stand against the devil's schemes."

Ephesians 6:13-

"Therefore put on the full armor of God, so that when the day of evil comes, you may be able to stand your ground, and after you have done everything, to stand."

Galatians 5:1-

"It is for freedom that Christ has set us free. Stand firm, then, and do not let yourselves be burdened again by a yoke of slavery."

We were created to not be conformed to this world but to stand apart. God wants us to be *in* the world, but not be *of* the world. In order to do that though, we have to learn how to stand. How do we stand? What are we standing against? The enemy wants to steal, kill and destroy us: our lives, our calling, our body, our relationship with God, etc. Anything that he can do to us, he will try. How do we stand against him or his schemes in our lives? We stand on the word of God and in His strength. The Bible tells us that in this world we will have trouble, but when chaos comes, we have a choice how we handle it, how we walk in it and what we stand against, if need be.

In order to do this there are things we need to keep in mind: 1-We have to recognize that we don't battle people, but the enemy. 2-You must train for battle and be taught how to stand when all chaos breaks loose in your life. 3-When the Lord frees you from a bondage, you have the strength to stand against it and not go back to the bondage it once held you.

When you get those three things in the right perspective, you will stand differently. God doesn't want you to walk around defeated. He already conquered it all for you, even death, for you! Get in His word, tap into His power and let Him teach you how to stand!

Love y'all! Have a great week!

Week 20

Happy Monday! This week I wanted to talk about being positioned! You were placed in this world for such a time as this! You were perfectly positioned to fulfill an important assignment!

The Word tells us in:

Esther 4:14b-

"And who knows but that you have come to your royal position for such a time as this?"

Psalm 138:8-

"The Lord will vindicate me; your love, Lord, endures forever—do not abandon the works of your hands."

Ephesians 2:10-

"For we are God's handiwork, created in Christ Jesus to do good works, which God prepared in advance for us to do."

All of us were created to do good works and God has known what they were since He created you. He made you knowing what purpose He created you for. He also knew what time and place to put you in to accomplish your mission.

Do not ever doubt if you should have been here or the time in which you live. The creator of all of the universe decided that this world needed you as well as all of the gifts and purposes that He put inside of you! Stand confident that you are here on purpose and filled with purpose.

He will not turn His back on what He has set for you to accomplish! Trust Him, lean into His will for your life and He will move through you!

Love y'all!
Have a blessed week!

Week 21

Happy Monday! Today I want to talk to you about Red Sea Rescues! We all face a Red Sea moment in life at one point or another. What do you do when you are standing in a place where you are pressed on all sides without a visible way out?

The Word says in:

Exodus 14:21-22-

"Then Moses stretched out his hand over the sea, and all that night the Lord drove the sea back with a strong east wind and turned it into dry land. The waters were divided, and the Israelites went through the sea on dry ground, with a wall of water on their right and on their left."

Psalm 34:19-

"The righteous person may have many troubles, but the Lord delivers him from them all;"

Malachi 3:6a-

""I the Lord do not change."

We are told in the Bible over and over that we are going to face challenges. We live in a fallen world with an enemy who seeks to destroy us. However, we are not left without hope. God shows us over and over how He rescues His people. He is the WayMaker!

The part that we can miss sometimes is that God doesn't change! If God did it in biblical times, He can do it now. If He delivered you from situations before, He will do it again. If He spoke something before, He will bring it to pass. He doesn't change! More than that, He is no respecter of persons. So He won't just do it for others, He will do it for you!

If you believe what He says, if you stand on His word, He will confirm His word over and over again in your life. If you find yourself in a Red Sea moment in your life, go to Him and His word, believe what He says, trust Him over the circumstances and watch Him work in your life.

Love y'all! Have a blessed week!

Week 22

Happy Monday! This week I want to talk to you about the Word becoming flesh!

The Bible tells us in:

John 1:1-

"In the beginning was the Word, and the Word was with God, and the Word was God."

John 1:14-

"The Word became flesh and made his dwelling among us. We have seen his glory, the glory of the one and only Son, who came from the Father, full of grace and truth."

John 3:16-

"For God so loved the world that he gave his one and only Son, that whoever believes in him shall not perish but have eternal life."

The Word that became flesh was Jesus. Jesus was not an "afterthought". He was with God from the very beginning and it was always in the plan to come here, share the truth of His father in love and give His very life to redeem us.

He came to live and experience a human walk so that He may relate to us and be able to fully comfort us in that there is nothing that we will experience in this life that He doesn't understand. He demonstrated His great love for each of us by giving His very life just to have us in heaven with Him. This living Savior that we serve gave it all for us and is always with us.

We should want to show our love for Him by living our life according to His plan. Live a life full of cultivating a relationship with Him and walking out the purpose He has for us. The word says that if we are His sheep we will know His voice and obey it. He gave everything for you, be willing to give your all to Him.

Love y'all! Have a blessed week!

Week 23

Happy Monday! This week, I want you to think about something: You serve an unrivaled, unmatched, unwavering, all powerful, living Savior! What's even greater? That same power is within you!

In the Word it says:
Jeremiah 10:12-
"But God made the earth by his power; he founded the world by his wisdom and stretched out the heavens by his understanding."

Luke 1:37-
"For no word from God will ever fail."

Ephesians 6:10-
"Finally, be strong in the Lord and in his mighty power."

We serve an awesome, wise, loving and powerful God! The whole world and everything in it, every detail, every process of how things work, was created at the sound of his voice. Then he gave Jesus the name above every name. There is NOTHING that can ever equal, rival, surpass, or be impossible in the name of Jesus. Nothing!

What is also truly amazing is that not only does Jesus have all authority, but when we enter into a relationship with him, he allows us access to his power!

He didn't leave us here to suffer and fumble through all the things that the enemy or this broken world throws at us with no help or hope to turn to.

Instead we are able to experience his power that is always readily available to us! So today and every day, remember who you serve! Have confidence in who he is and what he is able to do through you!

Love y'all!

Have a great week!

Week 24

Happy Monday! Today I want to talk to you about the vastly deep Love of our Father. His love is enormous, unfathomable, immeasurable, unwavering and never ending!

The Word says:

Romans 5:8-

"But God demonstrates his own love for us in this: While we were still sinners, Christ died for us."

1 Corinthians 2:9-

"However, as it is written: 'What no eye has seen, what no ear has heard, and what no human mind has conceived'— the things God has prepared for those who love him—"

Romans 8:38-39-

"For I am convinced that neither death nor life, neither angels nor demons, neither the present nor the future, nor any powers, neither height nor depth, nor anything else in all creation, will be able to separate us from the love of God that is in Christ Jesus our Lord."

The deep and unwavering love of God is too vast to even fully comprehend with our human minds. We can't even conceive how He could possibly love us as much as He does, yet He does. We spend a lot of our lives carrying guilt, feeling unworthy or unlovable; being afraid to step out into a full relationship with Him, because "how could He possibly love us", yet He does!

God isn't shocked by our actions. Once you go to Him and repent, He doesn't forever hold your sin against you. God doesn't label you by your sin, He calls you by your name! He knew from the beginning that we would fall, we would make mistakes that we ourselves could never reconcile. So in His great love for us and desire to have a relationship with us, He was willing to send Jesus to make the ultimate sacrifice for our sins.

We have the gift of knowing that He loved us enough, that we were worth it! We were worth stepping out of heaven and into time, living as our example and ultimately dying for! He loves you and nothing can separate us from His love! Accept His love today! Embrace it! Choose to let Him in! Choose to live your life as a thank you for all He has done.

Love y'all! Have a blessed week!

Week 25

Good morning! This week I want to talk to you about the importance of celebrating today! Each day is a day to be thankful for and rejoice over! Each moment is a gift!

The Word tells us in:

Psalm 118:24-

"The Lord has done it this very day; let us rejoice today and be glad."

James 4:14-

"Why, you do not even know what will happen tomorrow. What is your life? You are a mist that appears for a little while and then vanishes."

Ephesians 5:15-16-

"Be very careful, then, how you live—not as unwise but as wise, making the most of every opportunity, because the days are evil."

This week, and every day, it is important to celebrate! We don't have to celebrate in a way that is extravagant, but we need to remember that each day truly is a gift. When you get a revelation of how short time is (and the word makes this clear), then it is easier to celebrate them and not take them for granted. Sure you may get overwhelmed or concerned from time to time, but I hope that when you have those thoughts, you are able to take hold of them and shift your perspective.

Waking up to each new day is a gift that not everyone gets. Our days are numbered and time overall is short. Don't waste the time you are gifted wishing it away. Wake up excited! Be ready to enjoy the day! Seek how God can use you in every experience and make the most of every day that you are given!

Love y'all!

Have a blessed week!

Week 26

Good morning! This week, I want to encourage you to dig in and stay in! Distractions and discouragement come, but don't throw in the towel!

The Word says:

James 1:12-

"Blessed is the one who perseveres under trial because, having stood the test, that person will receive the crown of life that the Lord has promised to those who love him."

Galatians 6:9-

"Let us not become weary in doing good, for at the proper time we will reap a harvest if we do not give up."

Romans 5:3-5-

"Not only so, but we also glory in our sufferings, because we know that suffering produces perseverance; perseverance, character; and character, hope. And hope does not put us to shame, because God's love has been poured out into our hearts through the Holy Spirit, who has been given to us."

There are so many things that can come up in our lives that can pull us away from His presence and away from our relationship with Him! This is the enemy's game. If he cannot get you by temptations, he will get you so caught up in distractions or worldly things that it pulls you away from the Lord.

The enemy knows who God is and he knows that if we ever get a revelation of who God really is, he will not stand a chance!

I encourage you to fight for your relationship with God! Fight for an active move of Him in your life every day! Then no matter what comes your way, you refuse to let yourself be pulled away from your life source!

Love y'all!

Have a blessed week!

Week 27

Happy Monday! I want to talk to you this week about: Living in the Bonus! Did you know that you weren't just created to exist and "get through" the days? You were meant to live and fully!

The Word says:

John 10:10-

"The thief comes only to steal and kill and destroy; I have come that they may have life, and have it to the full."

Ephesians 3:20-

"Now to him who is able to do immeasurably more than all we ask or imagine, according to his power that is at work within us,"

Luke 6:38-

"Give, and it will be given to you. A good measure, pressed down, shaken together and running over, will be poured into your lap. For with the measure you use, it will be measured to you."

We are the most blessed people! We have the opportunity to live post resurrection! Jesus came to restore, redeem and give us access to direct relationship! I am so thankful to be living in the time that I am!

Jesus came not only to give us salvation, but there is so much more that we can experience now! The Bible is full of promises that God has spoken over us as His children. I don't know about you, but I am of the mindset that I don't want to just live to get through the day. I don't want to live in a way that I am just "suffering through it". I want to live in the bonus!

Salvation is the ultimate gift that we get to enjoy, but in the meantime, we can live in the bonus blessings He wants us to have as His children! I challenge you all to get excited about living and seek out everything that God has for you!

Love y'all! Have a blessed week!

Week 28

Happy Monday! This week, I want to motivate you to Walk in Power! You don't have to walk around with your head down and defeated! You have God on your side!

The Word says:

Colossians 1:10-11-

"so that you may live a life worthy of the Lord and please him in every way: bearing fruit in every good work, growing in the knowledge of God, being strengthened with all power according to his glorious might so that you may have great endurance and patience,"

Galatians 5:25-

"Since we live by the Spirit, let us keep in step with the Spirit."

John 15:4-

"Remain in me, as I also remain in you. No branch can bear fruit by itself; it must remain in the vine. Neither can you bear fruit unless you remain in me."

We as believers, do not have to walk around defeated or bound by worry, fear, or timidity. The word assures us that as children of God, we get the ability to walk instead, in His power. The Lord gives us the power to walk in His strength, His plan, His peace etc.

There is nothing that we can't face with Him by our side! We can therefore go out into our daily lives walking with our heads held high, knowing He is with us! The only way that we can walk in the things that He has for us, is by staying connected to Him.

He is our life giver, strength giver, life sustainer and we need to be sure that we stay connected each and every day. I encourage you to make time to connect with Him daily so that you are able to go about your lives walking in the power He gives us!

Love y'all! Have a blessed week!

Week 29

Happy Monday! This week, I want to talk to you about strength! There may be times where we feel weaker than others. There may even be times when we find ourselves weakened to the point that we are unsure how to keep moving forward. But God...

The Word says in:

Philippians 4:13-
"I can do all this through him who gives me strength."

Luke 1:37-
"For no word from God will ever fail."

Isaiah 41:10-
"So do not fear, for I am with you; do not be dismayed, for I am your God. I will strengthen you and help you; I will uphold you with my righteous right hand."

These verses are used often and I'm sure most can quote them. Sometimes they can become cliche and lose impact. I watched movies and videos depicting the passion scene of Jesus' life. Seeing these scenes spoke to me in a different way at times and I began to focus on Mary. I honestly don't think I can imagine what amazing inner strength she must have had.

Her faith no doubt played a role but just imagine for a moment some of the things she experienced. The unexplainable (to those around her) pregnancy where she must have been scared and unsure accompanied by the judgment she faced from others. The overwhelming task of raising the one and only son of God. Then having to stand by while your son is beaten to the point he is unrecognizable. Watch him suffer through the agony and carry his cross while she stood helpless. Then the unbearable task of witnessing him being hung on the cross and seeing him pass away while able to do nothing but sit at his feet. To me, it would be almost humanly impossible to handle all of those things and still keep your mind intact, even though she knew it was God's plan. However, this is a tragically beautiful way God shows us his power and the strength he can offer us.

No matter what you are facing in life, he can be your strength. He can enable you to withstand the seemingly impossible and do it all while keeping your mind and giving you peace in your spirit! If you find yourself feeling as if you can't bear something in your life right now, don't give up! God offers you hope, strength and peace! Just turn to him and his strength can get you through anything you are facing.

Love y'all! Have a great week!

Week 30

Happy Monday! This week, I want to encourage you to reach out beyond the four walls of your heart, your home, your church. Reach out and support those around you!

The Word says:

1 John 3:17- *"If anyone has material possessions and sees a brother or sister in need but has no pity on them, how can the love of God be in that person?"*

Luke 3:10-11- *""What should we do then?" the crowd asked. John answered, "Anyone who has two shirts should share with the one who has none, and anyone who has food should do the same."*

Matthew 25:35-40- *"For I was hungry and you gave me something to eat, I was thirsty and you gave me something to drink, I was a stranger and you invited me in, I needed clothes and you clothed me, I was sick and you looked after me, I was in prison and you came to visit me.' "Then the righteous will answer him, 'Lord, when did we see you hungry and feed you, or thirsty and give you something to drink? When did we see you a stranger and invite you in, or needing clothes and clothe you? When did we see you sick or in prison and go to visit you?' "The King will reply, 'Truly I tell you, whatever you did for one of the least of these brothers and sisters of mine, you did for me."*

Throughout the Bible we are instructed to help others. At times, it may be someone you know, others, it could be a stranger you come across or still other times when it may be a story of someone that you've heard about from others, but you may never meet personally.

There are so many different ways to help those around you both big and small! However, they all have one thing in common, each of them requires action!

Open your heart and your mind to the things around you, to the people and opportunities that God puts in your life. As you see a need arise around you, open your heart and ACT!

Love y'all!

Have a blessed day!

Week 31

Happy Monday! There are two things that God laid one my heart to share this week, but I want to start in scripture.

The Word says in:
Jeremiah 1:5-
""Before I formed you in the womb I knew you, before you were born I set you apart; I appointed you as a prophet to the nations."

Jeremiah 29:11-
"For I know the plans I have for you," declares the Lord, "plans to prosper you and not to harm you, plans to give you hope and a future."

Exodus 9:16-
"But I have raised you up for this very purpose, that I might show you my power and that my name might be proclaimed in all the earth."

The first thing that I want to share is this:
God knew you before you were ever conceived! He allowed you to be born at an appointed time because he has a purpose for you! Sometimes you may not feel great about yourself but if you are still here, God still has a purpose for you!

The second thing that I want to share is:
We all go through storms. No one likes them but they are a part of living and storms can have many reasons for being. They can be to teach us something, get rid of something in us, or show us God's strength in us. They can always bring us closer to God! They can plant a seed for your purpose. They can also be to bless someone else! Sometimes someone else needs to see you walk through a storm with God so that they can see God's power in your life.

No matter the reason, know that God always has a purpose for the storm, so seek him as the purpose as you walk through it. And always remember that you are a cherished child of God who has a purpose to fulfill for him!

Love y'all,
Have a blessed week!

Week 32

Happy Monday! This week I want to motivate you to walk in love!

The Word says:
Malachi 2:10-
"Do we not all have one Father? Did not one God create us? Why do we profane the covenant of our ancestors by being unfaithful to one another?"

Mark 12:31-
"The second is this: 'Love your neighbor as yourself.' There is no commandment greater than these."

Matthew 22:39-
"And the second is like it: 'Love your neighbor as yourself.'"

God wants us to love others, even those who are hard to love; forgive others, even those who are hard to forgive; and serve others, even those who are hard to serve.

None of us are perfect and we all are on different legs of our journey with God! There are times in all of our lives that unknowingly or not, we have found ourselves to be those hard to love, hard to forgive and hard to serve people. God, in His great grace, mercy and patience, walked alongside us to get us to a different space.

If you practice walking in these truths and walk in His words, you'll find that over time, you'll feel closer to in your walk by honoring him with your attitude and your actions.

Love y'all!

Have a blessed week!

Week 33

Happy Monday! This week, I want to encourage you to remember that you are an original! You are the only one of you that has ever and will ever be! Isn't that an amazing concept? There will never be another you! God chose you and sent you to do kingdom work!

The Word says in:
John 15:5-
"I am the vine; you are the branches. If you remain in me and I in you, you will bear much fruit; apart from me you can do nothing."

John 15:16-
"You did not choose me, but I chose you and appointed you so that you might go and bear fruit—fruit that will last—and so that whatever you ask in my name the Father will give you."

1 Corinthians 8:6-
"yet for us there is but one God, the Father, from whom all things came and for whom we live; and there is but one Lord, Jesus Christ, through whom all things came and through whom we live."

We are not put on the earth to just be wanderers until we leave. Each one of us has a reason for being here. When we get in touch with Jesus, He reveals to us our purpose that He put inside of us.

It's amazing that there are billions of people on the earth and each one has been given a unique calling that only they can walk out, but in order for us to walk it out, we have to stay connected to Jesus. We are His chosen and He is our vine, our lifeline. I have found that the closer I get to Jesus and the further He calls me, the more of Him I need and the more time with Him I need to spend. When I try to do things without Him, they don't work. Because without Him, I can't be fruitful for the work He has given me. Apart from Him I can do nothing. Things were designed that way.

Jesus knows more than we do. He knows what He has called us to do, what we will face and what it will take to accomplish these things and He knows what He is asking cannot be accomplished by us alone. We need His wisdom, His guidance, His strength, His provision, His peace, His reassurance and much more. We need Him!

When we stay connected to the vine, then our efforts will be fruitful. When we stay connected to Jesus, He will equip us with what we need. It is through Him that we have power, authority and provision to do what He has called us to do. Get connected and stay connected.

Love y'all! Have a blessed week!

Week 34

Happy Monday! This week I want to motivate you to get your heart back in it! We serve an awesome God! If you find yourself lacking zeal, possibly even just going through the motions, I encourage you to lean in, reconnect, and get your fire back!

The Word says in:
Job 11:13-19-
""Yet if you devote your heart to him and stretch out your hands to him, if you put away the sin that is in your hand and allow no evil to dwell in your tent, then, free of fault, you will lift up your face;you will stand firm and without fear. You will surely forget your trouble, recalling it only as waters gone by. Life will be brighter than noonday, and darkness will become like morning. You will be secure, because there is hope; you will look about you and take your rest in safety. You will lie down, with no one to make you afraid, and many will court your favor."

James 5:16b-
"The prayer of a righteous person is powerful and effective."

Jeremiah 29:12-
"Then you will call on me and come and pray to me, and I will listen to you."

Do you ever feel like you are praying out of habit, or that sometimes your heart just isn't really in it? When we find ourselves in that place, our prayers can lack power. The definition of earnest is: "adjective-resulting from or showing sincere and intense conviction."

The Bible says that when we are living a righteous life and we pray in this way with a sincere heart and intense conviction that our prayers are powerful and productive! I've heard it said a lot recently that sometimes we need to get desperate enough to cry out to God with this expectation and sincerity to see the results we are looking for. I agree! I have encountered things that have caused me to cry out to God and needed Him to intercede at that moment! Those taught me what an earnest/fervent prayer was.

We shouldn't have to be in those most desperate of moments to pray this way. Every time we come to Him it should be with an expectation for Him to show up! Sometimes it's an immediate intervention, sometimes it's a wait or just trust me but we should be listening and expecting His answer. It's important to pay attention to your attitude and your heart as you go to Him each time, it does matter. Pray with your whole heart; pray with urgency, expectancy and power!

Love y'all! Have a blessed week!

Week 35

Happy Monday! Today I want to talk to you about star lit vision!

The Bible tells us in:

Matthew 2:9-11-
"After they had heard the king, they went on their way, and the star they had seen when it rose went ahead of them until it stopped over the place where the child was. When they saw the star, they were overjoyed. On coming to the house, they saw the child with his mother Mary, and they bowed down and worshiped him. Then they opened their treasures and presented him with gifts of gold, frankincense and myrrh."

Luke 1:38-39-
""I am the Lord's servant," Mary answered. "May your word to me be fulfilled." Then the angel left her. At that time Mary got ready and hurried to a town in the hill country of Judea,"

Isaiah 6:8-
"Then I heard the voice of the Lord saying, "Whom shall I send? And who will go for us?" And I said, "Here am I. Send me!"

When the wisemen saw the star, they followed it. They acted out of obedience and they believed that the star would lead them to where they needed to be going. When the angel appeared to Mary and told her what was going to take place, she said "so be it". She had confidence that what the angel said was true and she quickly acted in obedience to prepare for what was coming. When Isaiah heard the voice of the Lord, he was ready to go in obedience.

God still speaks to us today. Are we willing to listen and act in obedience? Are we willing to walk in the path that He lights up for us? It can be easy to think "of course they obeyed, they are Bible characters". But we have to remember, they were people just like you and I. Yet they were able to put aside doubt and fear and walk in the things God had for them.

So I encourage you this week to examine your relationship with God. Do you have a starlit faith? Or are you only willing to go wherever feels comfortable?

Love y'all!

Have a great week!

Week 36

Happy Monday! This week I want to encourage you to be still and wait on God's timing! Stepping into the wrong thing at the wrong time, or even the right thing at the wrong time, can be worse than waiting! Hold on, God hasn't forgotten you!

The Word says:
Ecclesiastes 3:1-
"There is a time for everything, and a season for every activity under the heavens"

Ecclesiastes 3:11a-
"He has made everything beautiful in its time."

Psalm 130:5-
"I wait for the Lord, my whole being waits, and in his word I put my hope."

We live in a time where so much is available pretty immediately and it can cause us sometimes to be a little impatient. There are many different circumstances in our lives when we find ourselves wishing things would move along a little more quickly than they are. There are times when we may find ourselves in a difficult season and we just want it to be over as soon as possible. Maybe we've even prayed for something to take place that hasn't yet. Or perhaps God has given you a vision that just doesn't seem to be coming to fruition anytime soon.

Although it is natural to want to look ahead, we often are placed in a season of waiting for a reason. Time is never meaningless for Him and He never wastes a season! When we try to jump ahead, we may miss the very things God wants us to see while we are waiting. Or we may not learn the lessons that will benefit us or prepare us for the upcoming season.

God is not ignoring us when time seems to stand still. Instead, He loves us enough to keep us in the present, so that we may prepare for the season to come! So when you find God has placed you in a season of waiting, don't get discouraged. Seek what He would have you learn. Be still and be patient with God, He knows what He's doing and it's ALL about His timing!

Love y'all! Have a blessed week!

Week 37

Happy Monday! Today I want to motivate you to not throw in the towel! Tough seasons come, but we are not alone! The one who is within us, will help us overcome it!

The Word says in:
Joshua 1:9-
"Have I not commanded you? Be strong and courageous. Do not be afraid; do not be discouraged, for the Lord your God will be with you wherever you go."

Isaiah 41:10-
"So do not fear, for I am with you; do not be dismayed, for I am your God. I will strengthen you and help you; I will uphold you with my righteous right hand."

Deuteronomy 31:6-
"Be strong and courageous. Do not be afraid or terrified because of them, for the Lord your God goes with you; he will never leave you nor forsake you."

There are times in life that we feel alone. There may be times when we are going through a tough season and that it seems that no one else can relate. Trials come our way and sometimes there is nothing anyone can do to help the situation, other times, there may not even be anything that we can do to help change it.

But God!

His Word tells us over and over again to not be afraid or discouraged. He is with you and He is for you! When these moments or even seasons come, God doesn't abandon you! Instead, He walks WITH you THROUGH this difficult moment. Remember as you walk through this week, He is right beside you. Lean into Him and gain your strength from Him and His Words to you!

Love y'all!

Have a blessed week!

Week 38

Happy Monday! Today I want to encourage you to discover your worth! You are important! You are loved! You are worthy! Celebrate the One who celebrates you!

In the Word, it tells us:
Luke 12:7-
"Indeed, the very hairs of your head are all numbered. Don't be afraid; you are worth more than many sparrows."

Zephaniah 3:17-
"The Lord your God is with you, the Mighty Warrior who saves. He will take great delight in you; in his love he will no longer rebuke you, but will rejoice over you with singing."

Psalm 139:16-
"Your eyes saw my unformed body; all the days ordained for me were written in your book before one of them came to be."

There are times when we may experience things, are told lies about who we are, or have self-talk that discounts our worth. It is important not to hold on to that!

It is vital that we gain our worth from the One who created us! You are extremely important to God!

You are so important and so loved actually, that He concerns Himself with many details which you may be unaware of. How awesome is it that we serve a God who knows even the smallest details about each of us and loves us for who we are? He created you! He loves you! You were worth the creator of the universe taking His time to hand craft you and place purpose within you!

Take a moment to celebrate who you were created to be! Take time to express your gratitude to God for being personally involved in every area of your life!

Love y'all!

Have a blessed week!

Week 39

Happy Monday! This week I want to encourage you to push past your weaknesses! You are not alone in your weak moments!

The Word says:
Romans 8:26-
"In the same way, the Spirit helps us in our weakness. We do not know what we ought to pray for, but the Spirit himself intercedes for us through wordless groans."

2 Corinthians 12:9-
"But he said to me, "My grace is sufficient for you, for my power is made perfect in weakness." Therefore I will boast all the more gladly about my weaknesses, so that Christ's power may rest on me."

Matthew 28:20-
"and teaching them to obey everything I have commanded you. And surely I am with you always, to the very end of the age."

God knows that we have different weaknesses, He prepared us ahead of time by putting it in His word! However, there are still times that we can allow those moments to sometimes feel isolating. No matter what your weakness is, no matter how long you have found yourself in that space, remember that you aren't alone.

We are never alone!

There is nothing that we can ever do, or a weakness so great that we cannot overcome it with the Lord's help! Remember, you aren't fighting alone! We all have weak moments and we all go through some type of pain and suffering at some point or another. The good news is though, that God knows this.

He sees you right where you are and He has not left you there alone and without hope. He invites you to walk with Him and when you say yes to Him, He will be with you every step of the way!

Love y'all!

Have a great week!

Week 40

Happy Monday! Today I want to motivate you to face your tasks and challenges head on with your faith!

The Word says:
Matthew 5:41-
"If anyone forces you to go one mile, go with them two miles."

Colossians 3:23-
"Whatever you do, work at it with all your heart, as working for the Lord, not for human masters,"

1 John 4:11-
"Dear friends, since God so loved us, we also ought to love one another."

When we're given tasks to complete, or God calls us to serve, it is sometimes easier to take the path of least resistance! It is easier to stay in our comfort zone! However, it isn't always the way that God wants us to go.

We are called to do more! We are created to operate outside of what is comfortable. As His children, we are called to go above and beyond the task at hand! I encourage you to stretch! Go the extra mile to demonstrate the love we have for others.

Love y'all!

Have a blessed week!

Week 41

Happy Monday! This week I want to challenge you to not waste time or energy judging yourself or judging others!

In the Word it says:
Matthew 7:1-
"Do not judge, or you too will be judged."

Luke 6:37-
"Do not judge, and you will not be judged. Do not condemn, and you will not be condemned. Forgive, and you will be forgiven."

1 John 4:21-
"And he has given us this command: Anyone who loves God must also love their brother and sister."

Whew, this can be quite a challenge! We all have thoughts! Those thoughts can come from a variety of things including our past experiences, others' opinions and our perception of different things, but God has also given us the opportunity to decide what we continue to hold on to and what we allow to come out to others.

When someone else makes judgments about us, we fight it or we take ownership of it and let it define us. When we find ourselves judging others in our daily lives, that can lead to making comparisons to see how we measure up. These judgments can cause us to look down on ourselves or down on others. Our words hold power and these judgments can cause a wall to build up between us and the things God has for us.

We are not the perfect judge and in making our own judgments we overstep God's authority. Try thinking of some things you can do to stop yourself from judging others. Think of ways you can allow God to turn the posture of your heart to one of love.

Love y'all!

Have a great week!

Week 42

Happy Monday! This week, I want to encourage you to build a solid foundation for your life!

The Word says:
Matthew 7:26-
"But everyone who hears these words of mine and does not put them into practice is like a foolish man who built his house on sand."

John 8:47-
"Whoever belongs to God hears what God says. The reason you do not hear is that you do not belong to God."

James 1:22-
"Do not merely listen to the word, and so deceive yourselves. Do what it says."

There are many verses in the Bible that give us wisdom and insight into how we should live our lives. God loves us enough to prepare us for every situation that we may encounter. This guidance can be something that we take in and listen to or we can disregard it. If we have knowledge of how we are supposed to live and disregard that knowledge it is foolish, the Bible makes that clear.

As we build our lives, we have the choice to build it on the things that the world or our flesh would want, a foundation that can be unstable. Or we can choose to build them on the things of God, which are sturdy and unwavering. We should strive to build our lives on a solid foundation that will last forever, the Kingdom of God. Take a moment this week to evaluate yourself. What foundation are you building your life on?

Love y'all!

Have a great week!

Week 43

Happy Monday! Today I want to motivate you to push past the fear that can come up in your life!

The Word says:
Matthew 6:34-
"Therefore do not worry about tomorrow, for tomorrow will worry about itself. Each day has enough trouble of its own."

1 Peter 5:7-
"Cast all your anxiety on him because he cares for you."

Philippians 4:6-
"Do not be anxious about anything, but in every situation, by prayer and petition, with thanksgiving, present your requests to God."

We all come to places in life where things come up that cause us concern. If we allow it to, we can let these uncertainties take us to a place of worry. Take some time to think about where the core of the worry comes from.

At the very root of worry, is fear. Fear comes in many forms: the fear of the unknown, fear of failure, fear of the possibilities that things can go, fear of how it could even possibly work out. The root of fear is distrust in God. Distrust in what He can do and who He is.

If we let the fear linger too long, it can paralyze us from walking the path that God has for us and it can even chip away the peace and refuge we find in God. All hope is not lost! We don't let this fear overtake us or allow the worry to take up residence in our mind when the enemy decides to invade our thoughts. We can recognize them and bring them to the feet of Jesus. When we turn them over to Him, He will trade your worry for peace. Your anxiety for rest. Place your confidence in Jesus this week. Pray. Trust Him. Settle yourself and know that He will provide for you and bring comfort to you.

Love y'all!
Have a great week!

Week 44

Happy Monday! Today I want to encourage you to keep your eyes on God during difficult moments. All of us face difficulty from time to time, but we can choose to rejoice in the hope that Jesus gives us.

The Word says in:
Romans 12:12-
"Be joyful in hope, patient in affliction, faithful in prayer."

Psalm 30:5-
"For his anger lasts only a moment, but his favor lasts a lifetime; weeping may stay for the night, but rejoicing comes in the morning."

Hebrews 11:1-
"Now faith is confidence in what we hope for and assurance about what we do not see."

These verses are helpful nuggets that provide guidance to get us through those difficult seasons. As believers in Jesus, we have help and hope! It is a sturdy and confident hope.

We can confidently believe in the word which assures us that there may be times that are difficult, but those times are not our final condition, instead, they will come to an end! Even when we can't see the end, we can have faith in the future moment that we cannot quite see yet.

It's in the waiting for change that we can allow our minds to settle and our spirits lifted through prayer and praise. It is an awesome gift that we have as children of God, to know that in the midst of all of your difficulties and discouragement, there are two things you can be sure of: He will be with you and these moments will come to an end.

Love y'all!

Have a great week!

Week 45

Happy Monday! This week I was to encourage you to be a God-pleaser, not a people-pleaser!

In the Word it says:

2 Corinthians 5:9-
"So we make it our goal to please him, whether we are at home in the body or away from it."

Acts 5:29-
"Peter and the other apostles replied: "We must obey God rather than human beings!"

Psalm 147:10-11-
"His pleasure is not in the strength of the horse, nor his delight in the legs of the warrior; the Lord delights in those who fear him, who put their hope in his unfailing love."

Whether we know it or not, our lives are constantly in motion. If we are not intentional about our God-led goals, achievements, or accomplishments, it is easy to get swept away in the busyness of life.

The enemy will distract you any way that he can. He will do it through distracting your mind, your time or use the things that are in your mindset to feel the need to please people instead of God. There are going to be times when it feels that it is maybe better to please people. Or other times when pleasing God is directly the opposite of what the world would want for you to do. It's important to remember the ultimate goal is to please God.

Be willing to chase the God things in your life. Take a moment this week and think of these things. Who are you wanting to please most? What are you working towards in your life and is it pleasing to God?

Love y'all!

Have a great week!

Week 46

Happy Monday! This week, I want to motivate you to always keep growing! Growth is a continuous process that we should actively be striving for.

The Word says:
1 John 4:20-
"Whoever claims to love God yet hates a brother or sister is a liar. For whoever does not love their brother and sister, whom they have seen, cannot love God, whom they have not seen."

Romans 12:19-
"Do not take revenge, my dear friends, but leave room for God's wrath, for it is written: "It is mine to avenge; I will repay," says the Lord.

Proverbs 10:12-
"Hatred stirs up conflict, but love covers over all wrongs."

Having a relationship with God can put us on track for a continuous process of positive growth and development. If you are willing to submit your life to God and you are willing to continue to seek what He may want to show you each and every day, He will take you on a journey that is neverending. It is challenging but is so perfectly filled with grace. He will lead you step by step as you have the capacity to shift.

One key area we should constantly be stretched in, is caring for others. When you are filled with God's love, you will have a natural outpouring of love for others. You will be able to more easily see past others' shortcomings and still love them as God loves us.

As you go through today, ask yourself: Are you seeking growth in your spiritual walk or are you content where you are? Does your treatment of others demonstrate God's love or make you a liar?

Love y'all!

Have a blessed week!

Week 47

Happy Monday! This week, I want to talk to you about conviction!

In the Word it says:
Luke 6:46-
"Why do you call me, 'Lord, Lord,' and do not do what I say?

2 Timothy 3:16-
"All Scripture is God-breathed and is useful for teaching, rebuking, correcting and training in righteousness,"

Romans 2:4-
"Or do you show contempt for the riches of his kindness, forbearance and patience, not realizing that God's kindness is intended to lead you to repentance?"

Do you ever get a feeling that God is telling you to do something or turn away from something? That is called conviction. Sometimes, we are convicted to do things that are difficult. At that moment, we may want to run away. But when we run away, we are telling God that we would rather compromise than obey. We want the benefits of a relationship but when He asks us to obey Him, we are not willing to do the hard work.

Correction, teaching, reproof and training aren't always comfortable. However, they are necessary for our spiritual growth. If we want Him to truly be Lord of our life, the center of everything we do, we have to learn to listen and obey.

Take some time this week to think about these things. Are there any areas that you could be listening to Him better? What area(s) of your life is God convicting you to honor Him with?

Love y'all!

Have a blessed week!

Week 48

Happy Monday! Today, I want to encourage you to share your faith wisely! Being a witness for Jesus is something we should all be trying to strive for. However, we have to use wisdom, because there are situations where your thoughts, behaviors or actions can damage your witness for Jesus.

The Word says:
Romans 12:10-
"Be devoted to one another in love. Honor one another above yourselves."

Matthew 7:1-5-
""Do not judge, or you too will be judged. For in the same way you judge others, you will be judged, and with the measure you use, it will be measured to you. "Why do you look at the speck of sawdust in your brother's eye and pay no attention to the plank in your own eye? How can you say to your brother, 'Let me take the speck out of your eye,' when all the time there is a plank in your own eye? You hypocrite, first take the plank out of your own eye, and then you will see clearly to remove the speck from your brother's eye."

Luke 6:31-
"Do to others as you would have them do to you."

How sad it is to see Christians persecuting others for their religion or their sinful lifestyle. Of course, it's important to share our faith, but we need to do it as a light to others through love. Degrading others only discourages and angers them. This will further push them away from wanting to learn more about the love of Christ.

I encourage you this week to use your faith for good. Respect others and keep the golden rule in mind - love one another and treat them as you would want to be treated.

Love y'all!

Have a blessed week!

Week 49

Happy Monday! This week, I want to motivate you to dig into your Bible and really dig out who your father is! Get to know Him, not just for the "stories" but get to know Him deeply and personally. As you begin to dig out more of who He is, you will discover more and more about His capabilities.

In the Word it says:

Mark 12:24-
"Jesus replied, "Are you not in error because you do not know the Scriptures or the power of God?"

Psalm 119:11-
"I have hidden your word in my heart that I might not sin against you."

Philippians 2:10-
"that at the name of Jesus every knee should bow, in heaven and on earth and under the earth,"

Do you know what God is capable of? I mean really know? Past the things that just sound good at church or past the stories you have heard. Have you experienced His presence in your own life or read stories that He has allowed you to relate to in the Bible? There's nothing like reading stories in the Bible and being able to apply them to your life today.

God's word can guide, shape, help, encourage, and comfort us. Building your faith upon those who displayed great courage thousands of years ago honors God and His power. Don't make the same mistake as the religious leaders of Jesus' time. Spend time in the word for yourself. Allow Him to move in your life so that you may have your own testimony of all He has done!

As you begin this new week, think of ways to incorporate learning the scriptures in your everyday life so that you can apply them as the need arises.

Love y'all!

Have a blessed week!

Week 50

Happy Monday! Today I want to talk to you about food! Are you feeding yourself or do you find yourself starving?

In the Word it says:
John 6:35-
"Then Jesus declared, "I am the bread of life. Whoever comes to me will never go hungry, and whoever believes in me will never be thirsty."

John 4:14-
but whoever drinks the water I give them will never thirst. Indeed, the water I give them will become in them a spring of water welling up to eternal life."\

Matthew 4:4-
"Jesus answered, "It is written: 'Man shall not live on bread alone, but on every word that comes from the mouth of God."

Hunger for food is a feeling we experience every single day. It is usually something that we feel that reminds us we need sustenance to keep going. Jesus is our spiritual bread that sustains us and gives us the strength, guidance and wisdom to keep on walking in His path.

Do you have an internal reminder that lets you know when you are not being spiritually fed? If you aren't growing or maturing it may be time to make some changes in your daily routine, local church, or Bible study.

Love y'all!

Have a blessed week!

Week 51

Happy Monday! Today, let's talk about surprises!

In the Word it says:
Matthew 24:44-
"So you also must be ready, because the Son of Man will come at an hour when you do not expect him."

Matthew 24:36-
"But about that day or hour no one knows, not even the angels in heaven, nor the Son, but only the Father."

1 Thessalonians 5:2-
"for you know very well that the day of the Lord will come like a thief in the night."

Are you someone that likes surprises or do you like to know things ahead of time so that you are prepared? Have you ever walked into a class and heard the words "pop quiz"? If you have, it gives you one of two reactions. If you have been studying and listening then you feel prepared. If not, you feel panicked and wish you had some warning so that you could have better prepared. The same is true for us awaiting Jesus' return.

We have no way of knowing and won't have any warning when that moment will occur. Therefore, we must get ready, and stay ready. If you haven't made Jesus your Savior and Lord of your life, today is a great day to do just that! If you have, are you living your everyday life in a way that you would be prepared should He return without notice? If not, it's not too late to start! Begin today and continue to stay prepared!

Love y'all!

Have a blessed week!

Week 52

Happy Monday! For our last week in this book, I want to encourage you to be compassionate towards those that you interact with. Strive to show Jesus to those you encounter in your day to say life. You never know when that small act of kindness may make a major difference in someone's life. Let all you do, point others to Jesus.

In the Word, it says:

Ephesians 4:32-
"Be kind and compassionate to one another, forgiving each other, just as in Christ God forgave you."

Galatians 5:22-23-
"But the fruit of the Spirit is love, joy, peace, forbearance, kindness, goodness, faithfulness, gentleness and self-control. Against such things there is no law."

Hebrews 13:1-2-
"Keep on loving one another as brothers and sisters. Do not forget to show hospitality to strangers, for by so doing some people have shown hospitality to angels without knowing it."

Everyone you choose to do life with, everyone you meet from day to day, everyone that you pass by or interact with on any given day, has a life of their own that they are journeying through. Some points of the journey are more difficult than others and some journeys are more challenging than others, but we all are on one. Remember that.

Make a conscious effort to be kind to everyone you come into contact with. Be compassionate with people, you don't know the journey they are on or how it is affecting them. Forgive people for their shortcomings and actions that may have negatively affected you.

Jesus has been so gracious to us in forgiving and forgetting everything we have asked forgiveness for. Try to make an effort to do the same for others. Don't let the way others conduct themselves harden your heart or cause you to react in an equally hurtful way. Continue to strive to be calm, kind and compassionate, reflecting the love of Jesus as best you can. Forgive, heal, let go and move forward!

Love y'all!

Be blessed!

Thank y'all for taking this journey with me! I hope you have enjoyed traveling through this year together! I pray that you felt loved and encouraged, you felt stretched and challenged, most of all I pray you have grown during our time together!
~Love and Blessings~
Pastor Rachel

Numbers 6:24-26
""The Lord bless you and keep you; the Lord make his face shine on you and be gracious to you; the Lord turn his face toward you and give you peace.'"

About the Author

Growing up in Virginia, Rachel had a strong relationship with God from an early age. Through the years, he has led her closer to him and guided her to become a local church minister. During this journey, she created Courtesy Care and Creation Care ministries through her home church. Both of these ministries provided her with an opportunity to reach the community, grow in her faith and follow the nudge of God. After several years of ministering, Rachel answered the call to become a Pastor. Upon answering the call, she created her Rays of Light website, where she provides scriptures, devotions, testimonials and so much more. Rachel's mission is to use her calling to share, encourage, educate, and help others grow in their relationship with God no matter your background. Throughout this journey she has been an excellent example to her three wonderful sons, who enjoy learning the word and showing the love of Jesus to others with her daily. Currently, Rachel serves as Online Pastor at Life Changers Christian Center in Wytheville, VA. When she is not spending time with her boys, leading her local women's ministry, or co-hosting Faithful Light Podcast with her dear friend, she is creating content for Rays of Light. In the future, she hopes to continue to step out into new ventures as God lays them on her heart, and she is excited for the release of future books!

Contact the Author

Email: Raysoflight.info@gmail.com

Website: https://raysoflightinfo.wixsite.com/raysoflight

Facebook and Youtube: Rays of Light

Instagram: Raysoflight.info

Pick up your copy of Pastor Rachel's first book "Jumpstart Prayers!" on Amazon.com.

Please make sure to submit your testimony of blessing and healing you received from this book on the website to make sure it is featured. While visiting the site, be sure to subscribe to the website for newsletters, information and upcoming events. Prayer requests are always welcomed and prayed over daily.

Made in the USA
Columbia, SC
21 December 2022